SELF FOR DUCKS

How To Stay Calm On The Surface Whilst Paddling Like Crazy Underneath

By

Hannah Campbell

© Copyright – 2020 – Hannah Campbell

This book is dedicated to:

The 'feral pair'- my gorgeous blonde babies; I love you to the moon and back again. Thank you for making me the best duck I can be.

Contents

Introduction 1

PART I: Paddle Like Crazy 7

    Chapter One: Don't Get Stuck In the Pondweed 24

    Chapter Two: Calm on the Surface 49

PART II: Mixing It Up; In And Out Of Water 70

    Chapter Three: Flexible Paddling 71

Conclusion 83

Useful Things: 86

Acknowledgments 89

About the Author 91

Introduction

First off, thank you so much for purchasing my book. I know that there are many others out there right now – I've aimed to keep this short and sweet, with enough tools that you can quickly implement to make a real difference to feeling calmer. I hope it's something you will not regret, and perhaps we can have a chat about what you found useful or related to the most one day!

Secondly, you might be wondering – *WHY* Self Help For Ducks?

Well, nearly 10 years ago, a good friend of mine had come down from London to visit me after I moved out of the city and into the Essex 'countryside' (I'll use that term loosely, but fondly!). Following a night out exploring the local nightlife, and singing karaoke (badly, I might add) we walked the streets of my village to hunt down breakfast, hungover, sat ourselves down at the reservoir and we were watching the ducks. It was peaceful and the sun was shining across the water. What more could I possibly want? And I sat and looked at him and said:

"I'd quite like to be a duck ya know?"

And he looked at me with that confused look I've seen so many of my friends often give me when I've come out with yet another mad idea and I reasoned that

"Well – you see them swimming along the surface looking all happy and calm, but the thing is – underneath they're at it like crazy. I think I'm a little bit like that."
And Ben, being the man of many words that he is, agreed,

"Yeah, I guess you are mate." (He's a proper Londoner, so apply the accent for that)

So, I figure there are times where we all need to work like crazy, and times where we need to be cool, calm, and collected. And **sometimes,** a little of both. As millennials or whatever generation you may be, we live in a world where we are constantly on the go, needing everything to be done quicker, more efficiently, and with time and money constraints often feeling like barriers to getting everything done.

This book is for anyone who is looking to get more done, with less pressure and stress, would like some help getting in the right frame of mind to do so – and can relate to being a duck; calm on the surface but feeling a little frantic if you look a little deeper.

I've broken the book into three main sections, with actionable tips on how to make the best of being calm, super productive, and a blend of the two. As a single mum of two, trained in counselling and having run my own events company at the age of 15, been in and around the family business all my life – I'm confident to say **I have come across a thing or two that I found useful**; and hopefully, you will too. I've amassed some bizarre experiences, including being homeless and toxic relationships that lead to near mental breakdowns… and I have built myself up again on my own terms.

I may not be a doctor, or even have a degree (yet, it's on the to-do list!) – but I do have a head that is firmly screwed on enough to feel that what I have learnt in my short years of life has a degree of value to those of you who may find yourselves in similar positions. If I can do it – so can you.

Are you someone who has loads of ideas, but find yourself shrinking back when the idea of putting them into action comes around?

Wouldn't it feel great to just do it? You can. Without the fear of what others will think, or say.

You can start living your life exactly how you want to, in a way that works for you and makes you feel content. The more effort you put into your own life, the more you will get out of it. Ducks that invest in themselves, have the loveliest nests*.

As a busy mum, I have written this largely from the perspective of a woman and a parent because I can relate very well to both of those. Though you don't have to be either

of those to find this book useful –
the tips and skills are completely
transferable to everyday life,
whatever you are trying to achieve.
If you are constantly on the go, feel
the stress of life often has your legs
paddling like crazy underneath
whilst you are struggling to maintain
a cool appearance on the exterior
and would like to be able to get more
done and feel happier about it – get
reading and ready to change your
life for the better.

(*duck facts may be fabricated for illustrative purposes throughout the book)

PART I: Paddle Like Crazy

Why on earth would anyone want to paddle like crazy?

Loads of us have to be productive all the time though – as a single mum, I'm always on the go. And there are students, entrepreneurs, career climbers, guys with side hustles, mums with side hustles, anyone trying to finish big projects – a house renovation/ a garden restyle – whatever your reason is; I can bet it's because you want to achieve something MORE. You are striving for something **different.**

It may not be wildly different, just different from where you are right now in your current situation.

It's easy to get bogged down with the menial everyday tasks, the washing, going to work, come home, cook dinner, wash up, tidy the kitchen, pay the bills, maintain the house and the garden, go to the gym, bath, rubbish on TV/social media, bed, repeat X infinity.

Life gets busy. It's easy to see time fly past and you don't notice how many things you are taking on, until you begin to feel the weight of it, gradually becoming heavier, as your legs paddle faster and you keep smiling on the surface. Until you aren't smiling.

That was me – I was on my own, trying to juggle studying, being a mum to two children of primary school age, with very little support – and figuring out how to make a living.

At one point when my eldest was still at nursery, I tried to get back into the workplace to realise I was paying to be there after childcare costs!! But told that if I could wait six months I'd have enough of my own clients for it to be worthwhile. Who can do that?! Without family/friends offering help with childcare – and when you aren't qualified enough to jump straight into a position that pays enough, I often felt like I was constantly trying to climb but never really getting anywhere.

You might be able to breeze through that side of things and be lucky enough to have people around supporting you, but I'd hazard a guess that even then it still requires juggling. And organising things like a well-greased military operation.

A lot like a hamster on a wheel, putting in all that effort but never covering any significant ground. Desperate to change the situation I had found myself in, I would do courses that other people wanted me to do in an effort to be pleasing and progress – but I've since learnt, that if you aren't doing something because it's what you really want to do; it's incredibly difficult to stay enthused about it. I do however now hold qualifications in book-keeping. (I would not advise hiring me to do *any* bookkeeping though, as frankly, I am an awful bookkeeper.)

Is that something that you can recognize in yourself? Do you take things on because it's what other people think you should be doing? And so you go along with it because it feels like 'the right thing' to do? How much time have you spent doing things because someone else suggested it would be the best thing for you?

But somewhere along the line... it becomes a struggle, no

matter how much of a good idea it did seem, and yes it would fit in with your life/children/schedule... you aren't *really* into it. You don't love it. It doesn't match up with the picture in your head of what you would be doing with your life. So stop it? What would you really like to do? What would make you happiest? Maybe you have a talent for design, or you are really good at doing hair and would love to do bridal hair? Perhaps as a child, you'd always been really good at making things and have always fancied doing a tiling course to do mosaics and kitchen designs. Write them down. Break it into stages and figure out how you could incorporate it into something that fills a need or provides a service. If it's a service that people would be willing to pay for – it can be more than just a hobby. Once you've got that – you have to accept that it will take time to get good at it. Do the courses, ask people for help in improving that skill. Get as much experience as you can. Join online groups so that you have people in the same boat. But that's a whole journey on its own. For now – let's concentrate on how you are feeling.

Perhaps you sometimes feel like you have been trying to get things done – but no matter how hard you try, you aren't getting the results you want. And that can be frustrating, annoying, and ultimately bring you down. When you are constantly going uphill, keeping the motivation to climb can feel like a mountain of its own.

Unfortunately, I don't have a magic wand and I can't make it all better for you. You can make improvements yourself – if you put the work in to examine why you are feeling so stressed and actively put the effort into small changes.

Take the time to examine what is going wrong, and where your mindset is – you can change things, instead of repeating cycles of being super productive and crashing, or getting lots done but losing enthusiasm and feeling like the rest of your life suffers because you are going headfirst into only one area.

Balance is key – it's what I work with my clients on; finding a balance that works for them, to prevent mental health burnout, and to create a life that includes wellbeing in all areas.

So by no means do I suggest that going headfirst into six different areas will be helpful. You'll probably get burnt out, and end up hospitalizing yourself. Small, manageable changes – allow these changes to become habitual and then you can review and add more changes as you wish.

You can have a goal in mind. I find being able to picture an idea can be helpful. Some of my clients use mood boards to help them visualise what their ideal life would look like. If that involves two things and you feel that it's manageable – go for it.

Generally speaking, for most people having one key area that you are focusing on improving is much more likely to be fruitful than trying to become a professional ballet dancer and a world-renowned bricklaying babysitter who can juggle cats blindfolded.

Maybe the problem is different for you – and you want to start being more productive, but something is holding you back? I had a fear of not being good enough for ages. Even now it crops up, but the fact that you are reading this is probably a pretty good sign that I've thrown a whole chunk of that out of the window with some kind of reckless abandon akin to the women who thought burning bras was going to be a good idea. (It is not a good idea for me, aside from during a heatwave. Just for the record)

My fear of not being good enough stemmed from a childhood 'condition of worth' – and it takes time – and sometimes professional counselling to burn through these mental walls we have built up around what we can and cannot do. If you identify with not feeling good enough, or worrying what other people might think of you started doing 'your thing' or if you said what you really wanted to say – take five minutes to write down what the worst thing and the best outcome that could happen would be. If nobody is going to die – would you regret not doing it, more than you would be experiencing someone else feeling uncomfortable? If it could possibly make you really happy – what is stopping you? Life is short.

The negative thought patterns that can surround our self-image and belief are often ideals that other people have placed upon us as we grow up, and even as we forge our first steps in the professional world or parenting world. The bottom line is – you CAN do, whatever the hell you like. It doesn't mean that you always should, but the fact is that you CAN.

If you struggle with believing in yourself – or have been bullied at some point into believing that you can't do something/aren't good enough/should leave it to those who could do it better – try and identify where that thought comes from, and then build up your own personal memory portfolio of your positive achievements find a time or event where you did something really well – how did it feel? There must be at least one occasion. If you're struggling, start with really small things and build up – did you make an amazing cup of tea for a spouse or colleague? What about a really good dinner? Did you ever get home in record time and beat all of the traffic and feel smug about it? Yes?!

Brilliant. Maybe you finished a college course or exam? Small triumphs can domino into big ones. When you feel the negative thoughts creeping in – go through some of your positive ones and remind yourself of the achievements, wins, obstacles that you have overcome.

There is no right or wrong way to go about getting more done and working hard at it – the best way for one person, will not be the best for another. You simply have to find what works for **you**. Whatever that may be. For instance, I'm a very visual person – so I hang **VERY** large reminders for myself (even when writing this book, I've had a poster-sized to do on my kitchen cupboards with my self-imposed deadline count down each month!) You may react better to digital planning apps on your phone, to-do lists, it is just a case of trial and error – and then sticking with it.

I can promise you though that your life will change because of it. Once you find a method that works for you and dig your heels right into it, traction will be gained. Improvements will be made. And that *will* feel good.

I'm going to go into some of the reasons why having the wrong mindset will stop any amount of physical effort from getting you where you need to be – and vice versa, even with the right mindset if you aren't making enough physical efforts, you will still find yourself stuck and that feels like crap, which in turn will leave you feeling demotivated and miserable.

You deserve to achieve what you want to. You honestly don't have to stay stuck. You can if you want to. Carry on doing things the same as you are now and just get by, feeling slightly annoyed that Nicole got the promotion and Mark proposed to his girlfriend after buying himself a new car and you're... well, you're still not where you wanted to be?

Getting unstuck might feel better than that. It might feel freeing. Empowering even. And yes it might take a while – but what else are you doing with that time? Cliché it might be – but anything worth doing will be worth the work and the time. I probably sound old and boring saying that, but it really is. You can sit around and wait for a mystery benefactor to change your life or a miraculous lottery win, **or** you can take steps towards changing your own life.

Chapter One: Don't Get Stuck In the Pondweed

"Be like a duck. Calm on the surface, but always paddling like the dickens underneath." ~ **Michael Caine**

Sorting Out Your Mindset

Did you know that your thoughts, affect your feelings – which in turn, affect your behaviour?

You may or not know that this comes from Aaron Beck's CBT – Cognitive Behavioral Therapy. And it holds some serious weight behind the theory that if you change how you think about something, you will ultimately change how you feel about it. And in turn – when you change how you think and feel, your behaviour will change too.

So – more positive thoughts = positive feelings = positive actions/behavior.

You don't have to become a ray of sunshine or a beacon of zen. But by identifying the thoughts that are causing you the most stress, or hindering your progress is going to be key in moving forwards with a bit more spring in your step and a little less chaos.

What puts you off doing what you really want to do? Do you put pressure on yourself and then end up not doing it in case it ends up 'wrong' or not 'good enough'?

If you can, get a piece of paper and write down the things you normally tell yourself or others as to why you aren't doing what you want. Some of the things my clients tell me include –

I don't have enough time, I'm too busy, I don't know enough about it, I need someone else to help me, Why would I want to do something I'm not good at? I'm probably going to fail anyway, There's already loads of other people doing it, What's the point – I probably won't do anything after it anyway...

9 times out of 10 – There is something that can be done about them. Or they just need reframing more positively. Break it down and make time, ask for help where required, what would need to happen for you to be able to turn it into a positive or can do?

A reframe might look like "*I don't have enough time **alone, but I'll ask a babysitter to come on Wednesdays to get a couple of hours to myself***".

Take some of yours and see if you can turn them on their heads to work for you. The more you practice doing this when they come to mind, the more habitual it will become to turn things into a positive so that your situation works **for** you rather than against you.

It sometimes really is a case of ditching the fear or embrace the fear and just doing it anyway. I took a motorbike lesson last month because I've always wanted to get my bike license – I kept telling myself (and listening to others who told me the same) that I shouldn't be riding a motorbike because I have kids/because I'm a woman/because I already drive a car... but truthfully; I'd much rather be a role model to both my son and daughter – I tell them that they can do anything they set their minds to, so would I want them to shy away from doing the things that make them happy? Yes, it could be dangerous, but so could crossing the road.

The last thing I would suggest that is really important to anyone who wants to suddenly make a big shift in the level of productivity – is to be able to clearly identify WHY you want to push yourself. What is it that on a deeper level that truly motivates you? Some coaches will refer to this as finding your 'WHY'. Without having a reason behind why you are doing all the things you are, what is it that keeps you paddling? Why not just float, or stay on the edge of the pond not getting anywhere. As a parent – it's quite often family that is a big motivator – the want and need to provide, to achieve security, to set an example to children. As a single person, it could be to prepare for having a family, to be able to have adventures and go travelling, to gain some financial security, to expand your knowledge and experience to build a better career, business, or lifestyle.

<u>A really interesting, but slightly morbid; if you will, exercise to reflect on this:</u>
– Lay down. Close your eyes. Take a moment to breathe and relax and then try the following:
Picture yourself, at the end of your life's journey. You've lived a long life, many years from now. Imagine that everything has gone exactly as you wanted it to. It's been a good

life. You were happy and content. You did exactly as you set out to. What will it look like? What will you have achieved? What do you want to be remembered for? What were your biggest achievements? How will people think of you?

What kind of answers did you come up with? Did you manage to get a degree? Did you travel the world? Perhaps you watched your children get married and were able to save enough to set them up with driving lessons, a college/university fund, or a house deposit. Did people think of you like a really helpful person? You were able to look after your elderly relatives because you'd become your own boss and could work flexibly around other commitments. Whatever it was – make a note of what you had imagined and use it to keep you on track somehow, whether it is sticking pictures up, writing a note to yourself on an alarm that goes off every so often, in your diary, inside the fridge door, hiring someone to call you up once a month and remind you – I'm sure you can think of something. Having a clear vision of where you want to end up can help to become clearer on the steps needed to get there. Go back to this exercise as and when you need to refocus on that end goal.

Practical Ways to Get Across the Pond

Now that you've spent a little time identifying what is preventing you from thinking in a way that enables you to paddle like crazy when you need to, it's a good time to figure out **how** you will paddle like crazy. Maybe you've got things you already do and they are working for you. Brilliant. If not, make notes, try things, refer back to the book, ask a friend who seems to be super busy whilst being calm on the surface how they manage it – and find what works for YOU. (You may also discover that they really aren't as calm as you think)

How do you organize your time? (Do you even organize your time?!) I'm going to put a link to a blank block diary that you can use in the resources part of my website that you should be able to get to from reading this book. The principle of blocking out time just means that you can schedule things – it doesn't have to be exact, for those of you with tiny humans; I get it, life can be unpredictable. One minute everything is running on time, the next – shoes are missing, bags aren't where they should be, the dog is sick on the carpet and you've lost half a morning!

But when you turn something into a habit, it is much MUCH more likely to get done routinely and will eventually take less effort to complete because you just get on with it. (Do **not** schedule too much, to begin with, if you aren't currently – you don't want to be overwhelmed). Start with the area that you really want to improve first, implement one thing at a time and build on it. If you are not a morning person – start with a morning routine and just do three things. Your morning routine can even start the night before by ensuring you have things laid out or put away/breakfast set up in advance. Maybe you want to get better at sorting your bills and admin out – focus on that habit for a couple of weeks, once you've nailed it, add something else to your routine, and so on.

Some people find that short, intense bursts of really hard, focused work with planned rests, and rewards keep them motivated. (I'm one of those – I have a tendency to procrastinate!) I use a Pomodoro timer and to-do list app when I have a lot on – this is brilliant for revision too. For those that may be wondering why I'm talking about Italian tomatoes: A Pomodoro is a measurement of time originally used by Francesco Cirillo,
his technique uses a timer to break down work into intervals, often 25 minutes in length. I simply mark how many Pomodoro's I expect something to take, short loo/drink breaks between each one, and after a set of 3 or 4, I take a bigger break.

When working on something and using Pomodoro's – switch off distractions/notifications/social media. There are plenty of apps available that can help with this – or just an old school kitchen timer that you twist and pop on the desk or kitchen side is fine! I started using this technique when I was studying to get essays done and realized it works pretty well with most tasks if I need to sit down and focus.

If you can dedicate bigger chunks of time to tasks or you have projects that you will throw yourself into for several days – set alarms on devices with reminders or deadlines. Having a set time to accomplish something by can be a huge motivator – but if you are also a fan of the snooze button – rope in a friend, workmate, random stranger to hold you accountable. Join an online group where you can post about it and ask someone in there to give you a shout and make sure you are on track.

Who are your ducks?

Having people to hold you accountable as an adult is important, and makes getting things done that little bit easier – as children you have your parents, teachers, club leaders there to keep you on the path you are meant to be following but as adults you just get left to your own devices! And it's scary sometimes, life has no manual after all.

If you can afford to get a coach or therapist I'd highly recommend it. As a disclaimer – I'd recommend getting some talking therapy in the same way that I'd suggest getting your car serviced yearly. We take such good care of our vehicles, if they run low on fuel, we dash to a petrol station, so why not do the same for ourselves? (Something to ponder for another day perhaps)

If getting private help is currently out of reach – make a pact with a trusted friend to support each other. Join a group online for whatever it maybe you are working on. There are groups, websites, and forums for all manners of subjects now – that is one beauty of the age of technology. If you can't join a real-life club or community to be in touch with people with similar interests than you can definitely find one online. If you can't find one – build one!

On the flip side – if there are people who are draining you or giving you some of the reasons that were affecting your mindset – remove them. REALLY. One of my counselling peers used the phrase "drains and radiators" and at the time, I found this quite funny, but it sparks a little truth, some drain from your life, others radiate good energy.

When others around you detract more than they add to your

life, consider why you are keeping them around or allowing them to cross boundaries where you end up feeling uncomfortable, sad, or hurt?

      Do you feel bad about saying no to them or is the idea of moving forward without them something that makes you feel sad? You are not responsible for them; unless they are your children. However you want to put it: distance yourself, take a step back from (a giant leap if needed), cut yourself off, and finally, if still causing more damage than good make a choice about cutting them out. When you are pushing yourself, or under everyday stress, the last thing you need is someone who wants to pull you back; whether they are doing it consciously or not. (I like to believe that people are, inherently good. Most people aren't consciously trying to make you feel bad, they just have their own stuff going on – but that doesn't mean you have to allow it to drag you down) You can always reintroduce yourself when you have the energy to spare should you choose to.

Where are you most productive?

If you are trying to set up a small business or study around other commitments, it can be really difficult to have time or space for yourself, especially as a parent.

If you are more of a 'doing' person – set up a space that you physically have to move yourself to, or drive to a coffee shop away from your usual surroundings if it is possible. The act of actually disconnecting from the normal will mean that you **have** to get things done. No browsing the internet, scrolling through social media. Set yourself three tasks. Get on with it. You really will feel miles better for it.

Finally – if you are running around with kids or work during the day and find that by the time the evening comes you just don't have the energy or inclination to be doing anything else at that point. Get up earlier and do up to 3 things in the morning. Maybe just one. But ultimately – dedicate at least twenty minutes to doing something for yourself or one of the jobs you hate before anything else gets done. There's a famous Mark Twain quote that says "if you eat a frog first thing in the morning it will be the worst thing you do all day." You'll find you make incredible progress if you can find just a small chunk of time at the start of each and every day when you still have the energy to focus and apply yourself fully before the daily grind has eaten away at your soul!

Chapter Summary/Key Takeaways

Sorting the mind you need to:

- Figure out what reasons you are giving yourself for not doing what you want

- Turn them around and reframe them into a 'can-do'

- Figure out what truly makes you want to push and how to use it to stay motivated – Find your WHY

To get more done we need to:

- Reach out for support

- Surround yourself with people that add to your life, not detract from it

- Trial methods that work for you – scheduling, timers, alarms, removing negative people, becoming an early riser, using routines

- Make a space – Move to a different space – Get stuff done

- Dedicate even just 20 minutes a day to do something for

yourself, small progress is better than no progress at all

In the next chapter, I'll cover some of the things I do to stay calm on the surface – whilst implementing what you've managed to do to 'paddle like crazy'. It's important to have a little balance – if all you did was speed through life at 100miles an hour, you'd probably end up having some kind of breakdown, or repeatedly find yourself at the point of burnout – trust me, not fun. There is nothing glamourous about burnout; it can affect any of us. Take the breaks, take care of yourselves. At the end of the book, I'll include a list of links resources and other useful books so that you can access everything online. You can even email me (should you choose to. I mean, you don't have to. I'm not going to make you – I'm a little weird, but not *that* weird).

Chapter Two: Calm on the Surface

"Always behave like a duck- keep calm and unruffled on the surface, but paddle like the devil underneath."
— **Jacob Braude**

If you've made it this far, you may have begun to realise that I can be quite a hyper – if not 'intense' kind of person at times. <u>But</u> – I am human. And so are you. When you are putting your all into anything, be that raising tiny humans, starting a small business, training for a marathon or other sports – it's easy to feel overwhelmed! Especially if you are a little bit crazy and doing a combination of the above on your own!

There are so many reasons why people feel bad about doing less – ironic when I've spent the last chapter talking about doing more; it's also more than okay to do less sometimes. With a lot of my clients – my work is showing how doing less can enable them to do more. When you step away from the business, or from your day to day tasks – you allow your brain to subconsciously process and almost rehearse what you need to do so that when you return to it – you are more able to approach the task with renewed vigour and a new perspective. (Why do you think musicians don't practise 24 hours a day, 7 days a week?)

With social media being such a huge part of our lives now there are endless opportunities to have the 'perfect' lives shown to us.

Not one single person has a perfect life, 'normal' (for lack of a better word) people do not live in show homes all day long, those polished pictures of clean children in milky white kitchens beaming joyous little smiles have probably been taken countless times to get the shot so please do not give in to the pressure to think that your life should look like X Y or Z. Everybody has faults, flaws, little quirks. But it will not all be shown on the front page of the carefully curated social media that you see daily.

Your life can look however you want it to if it feels good to you that *really* is all that matters. Nobody else will be going the same way through life as you, the only person who will be looking back on it all, is you.

When you are trying to improve your life, your situation, or simply just your rate of productivity – you can end up feeling restless, bored, and unenthused about constantly having to do the same stuff, over and over again for a long period. It can be dull. Frustrating. Infuriating at times. You might feel tired, fed up, drained. Maybe a cocktail of all of the above. So find a way to recharge, to fire yourself up to be able to stay calm on the surface, feeling good and able to continue tackling whatever waters may be headed your way.

Nest & Rest

What do you feel like at home?

I'd vouch for making sure there is a place or space within your home where you can feel completely and utterly relaxed, and shut off from the world. Very much like I said in the previous chapter about having a place that you can get things done, it's just as important to have a place to switch off. Even – if it's just for ten minutes every now and then. Your home is your sanctuary, your safe space from the hustle and bustle of the outside world. For those of you with children, you may remember when you set up a baby's nursery wanting it to feel calm, soothing, reassuring – because the world is a big, loud, scary space. I'm suggesting that even as adults – it's a brilliant idea. Who wouldn't want somewhere that is calm, soothing, and reassuring? (I recently cleared out my understairs cupboard, and after emptying it, just sitting in a small, white space – was blissful. Though I obviously can't keep my wizard-like retreat forever!)

Having somewhere you can retreat to as and when necessary is a great way of just stepping out of the action and recharging ready to keep going. What could your space be? A nice chair in the corner of your living room to read in? Maybe you like a soak in the bath? If you are more of an outdoor person could you create an area in your garden to sit in the evenings, with some lights, and nice plants?

Make a point of having space, small or large that is your refuge.

Scheduling rest. This is almost essential if you intend to be able to push yourself at high levels for increased periods, if you are caring for children alone, or studying. Even if you are just a single person who is working and studying or running a side hustle – We are not superhuman, just simply human.

Nobody can function on turbos forever without stopping. Your body and mind will need a rest. Much like an athlete who may train several times a week, they will still have rest days and even a whole 'off-season'. Would professionals take resting so seriously if it wasn't important? So why don't you allow yourself the proper opportunities to rest?

Resting doesn't have to look like a nap and a long sleep. Resting can take all sorts of forms – again it is about finding what works for you. Maybe you need time away from people in the quiet reading a book, or the complete reverse – a noisy night out in a bar with friends that you've not seen for months catching up and singing along to dodgy 80s power ballads. Whatever makes you feel refreshed and ready to go is completely okay. It doesn't have to be recommended or approved of by anybody else but you; because it is *your* break. Not anybody else's.

Part of being okay with doing less – for those of you with already incredibly busy lies or with a bucket load of responsibilities; is knowing that whatever pace you can comfortably maintain in *your life* is okay. It's a bit like running a marathon alongside the professional runners – you simply cannot expect to maintain the same pace – you are most likely not built the same, nor supported by a dietician, personal trainer, and a sponsorship team. You are one human – just do your best. That doesn't mean that you can't train, use the resources available to you, learn more, and improve. It just means that it's perfectly acceptable to do things in your own time, around your family life and other commitments – as long as you are pushing ahead and making small steps – you will cross the finish line too.

 Along with resting – being able to identify when you need a little care and attention for yourself is really important. How often do you stop and do something for yourself? As a single parent, this can be difficult depending upon how much support you have or time for yourself. Grab a pen and paper, and make a list of things that you can easily do for yourself, along with things that may take a little more time. This could include things as simple as:

-Taking a bath
-Going for a walk (with or without a dog!)
-Following a yoga video or other exercise. There are plenty to be found online now, so no excuses!
-Making yourself your favourite food

-Have a pamper session: manicure/pedicure/book a massage etc.
-Read a book with a glass of wine

I know that they are simple – but sometimes that really is all it takes.

Just make actual time for yourself; it sets a good example, it continues to show yourself that you care for yourself.

Learning to Let Go

This one is pretty self-explanatory, but I can't really stress it enough. Letting go and being okay with letting go is so important to self-growth and moving forwards in your own life.

Can you think of at least one or two things or people you haven't allowed yourself to let go of; despite knowing they bring nothing positive to your life?
If you don't give yourself permission to let go you will waste too much time, energy, and money on bad people, bad times, and bad... food?!
You mostly cannot control other people or things. And spending time and energy on unrealistic expectations of others will rob you of time you cannot get back again, leaving you disappointed, drained, and worn out. When you could feel better, and move towards a life

where you feel calmer, more relaxed, and fulfilled.

You can control yourself. Going back to the same CBT theory that I mentioned at the very beginning of the book – your thoughts affect your feelings which affect your behaviour – you might not be able to influence anyone else, but if they are harming you; if you aren't able to think positively about it and it is draining you – cut it out or reduce it and replace it with something that makes you feel good, inspires you, allows you to be the best version of yourself.

It might seem really brutal at first to cut off what could be perfectly functional friendships at a glance – but think about the people who make you feel tired with every exchange, those that are only on the end of the phone because they want something from you, but never call or answer when the shoe is on the other foot; we've all encountered them. It is okay to say no. Even clients can do this in business – overstepping professional boundaries, asking for things outside of the remit of your professional relationship. It is okay to stop feeling like you should help them out. Your time and energy are precious – reserve that kind of treatment for your nearest and dearest. For those that are there for you. For those that are paying for your time or services appropriately.

Think about how the weight will be lifted from you – how good will it feel not be indebted to others who you have no actual responsibility for?

How will you feel when you can comfortably put your foot down when it's time to leave because you have things that *you* want to do or are paid to do instead of getting dragged into someone else's commitments because you would previously just stayed as saying no felt awkward. It's not being unkind, it's just being focused on what is important at that moment in time. And that's not to say I'm against helping people – it feels good to help others, and that's partly what stops most of us from saying no.

But when you are feeling drained, or cajoled into doing things; it's okay to just remove yourself from those situations, even just for a while so that you can better focus solely on improving yourself and your own life.

Have you been stuck in a job that you don't enjoy anymore or aren't progressing in? What is stopping you from leaving? Could you look for another one? Do it. Don't wait for 'the right time', if you need to, ask if there is an opportunity to move up – how could you help that happen? Are there any courses or skills you could develop to do so? If you don't ask – you don't get. It is often that simple. But don't stay stuck for the sake of staying. It will wear you down and life is simply too short to feel so exhausted when we spend such a large portion of our time working.

It's a little bit morbid, but I have an extension in my internet browser to show me how much time I have left if I live to be 85 – every time I open a new tab, I see the circles getting coloured in. It keeps me motivated.

Finally – one of the biggest keys to being calm on the surface and feeling positive – is having a good support network. You will **never** see a duck alone.* they always seem to be in groups, or huddles, or they have a little duck friend with them. It takes a village to raise children. It takes a team to play a game of football. There are people behind the scenes on TV and Radio shows. In the West End, there are make-up artists, wardrobe teams, lighting, and sound 'crews'.

Find your village. Build a team. Whether it is made up of friends and family, or hiring a cleaner (I did this for the first time recently – best money I've ever spent on myself. Was amazing) Outsource what you can afford to. Pay a babysitter or swap an evening with a friend.

(*I have not researched this. You may see one, one day. Please don't sue me.)

Key Takeaways

- Your energy is your biggest resource. Do not waste it.

- Let go of the things you can't change – including people, relationships, clutter.

- Self-care is vital.

- Build your support network with good ducks.

In the next part of the book, you can take everything you've done so far – the tools and mindset to paddle like crazy, the idea of being able to remain calm on the surface and nurture your own feel-good energy and combine them to be able to mix it up and maintain that as a balance.

PART II: Mixing It Up; In And Out Of Water

Chapter Three: Flexible Paddling

"I don't think you're happier if you're thin or beautiful or rich or married. You have to make your own happiness. My heroines do not become beautiful elegant swans, they become confident ducks and get on with life." ~ **Maeve Binchy**

There inevitably needs to be a combination of paddling like crazy and keeping things calm on the surface to sustain growth – AND – more importantly, retain some kind of even keel and balance.

If you only toil, graft, and grind day after day after day, you will wear yourself into the ground. If all you are doing is 'taking it easy' or waiting for things to happen – frustration will kick in, tiredness and apathy will take over and make it harder to get the wheels turning again.

Things will change, you will adapt. And much like the weather around the duck's ponds with each season; life can be seasonal too and you will have times that are busier than others where heavier workloads are put upon you and it will only be by *choosing* to take control and try different things that you can grow with change.

It requires creative thinking and a whole ton of flexibility at times when life is busy. But just like the duck – go with the flow at these points in time.

Have you ever found yourself getting annoyed that things don't fit in with the schedule you'd sorted in your mind? Or been unwilling to bend to be able to fit something else into your already chaotic week? Go back to the previous sections – how can you make it happen? How can you make time? Is there someone that could help? Do **not** be afraid, or too proud to ask for help. Having that team of people on your side will be the key to continue being able to adapt and grow in those situations.

Be Your Future Friend

I know this may seem like common sense, and I don't want to teach you to suck eggs. But, a little preparation goes a long, long way.

When you plan things in advance and prepare for them – it cuts out decision making, which uses a lot of cognitive energy. There are reasons why some of the most influential people will always be seen wearing the same outfits/give or take a tie change. (ever noticed this?) It is because by wearing the same thing almost every day, they cut out a decision to be made – saving that little bit of brainpower for more important things. It's said that on average, as a human you make a staggering 35,000 decisions a day – conscious ones. So if you are making such a high amount of decisions – it'd be fair to say that minimizing the bigger choices will leave you with a better amount of critical thinking time and energy rather than getting decision fatigue before you have achieved the things that are actually important to *you.*

One of the easiest things you can prepare in advance to cut down on time wasted making minor choices include food – prepare a meal plan and shop to that, not only will it cut down on wasted food; which is always a bonus, it will enable you to stick to a budget if needed, and you will know what is ahead for your week. If I'm working with a food plan, I tend to have a couple of 'cupboard' meals that are flexible in case things need moving around. Food is an easy choice to remove, you have to eat every single day, so you know that it's going to need doing.

Going back to the outfits – you know that you are going to wear clothes each day (I'd hope... unless that's your thing. You flaunt that, I'm not judging) so lay them out the night before, it will cut one of the biggest decisions you make in the morning and allow you to get dressed immediately and begin your day without having to make sometimes multiple decisions – ladies (and men, I'm not being sexist here); I've done it, and I'm pretty sure you probably have too, gotten dressed, no it's not right, change, change again! Cut that wasted time out and decide the night before. It will make you feel amazing when you can just slip the prechosen clothes on. Like you are a super decision making machine! If you really feel like going the extra mile to simplifying this choice – par down your wardrobe and begin a capsule collection in three colours, everything will go together, I spent a year or so wearing only black pink, and grey with some white. Granted, I also had pink hair at the time, but boy did it make life easy. Everything I owned matched to everything else with ease. It was blissful!

Simplify as **MANY** things as possible. Where else in your life could things be made less complicated? Do you own duplicates of things – kitchen items/clothes/shoes/kids toys/cd's/blankets/suitcases – All of these things take up mental space, physical space if you've got more than one or two items that do the same job; get rid?

A little harsh maybe, but it cuts down on confusion, cleaning, tidying. There are loads of organizing systems that are quite 'fashionable' for want of a better word now. I'm a big fan of 'that Japanese one' (can I name it?) – I have by no means perfectly executed organizing my belongings, but really helps to par down your possessions and live more simply. Not only does it make finding what you are looking for easier, but the old adage that a clear space is the equivalent of a clear mind had certain truths to it.

Dangerous Ducking Around

There are certain traits that ducks have that aren't always helpful.

Ducks are often found with their heads underwater, but the real danger is if you don't come up for air and see what is really going on, you can't know what problems you're really dealing with.

By this – I mean, that when you're deep in the pond, and you've been there for ages – sometimes it takes a walk away to dry land to gain some perspective.

How else can you see what the problem is if you are only looking through the same pond-weed every time?

If you are still struggling to figure something out or feeling dragged down by a situation. Stop. Take yourself out of the pond, start using a journal, reflect upon your feelings, and if you feel the need, speak to someone from a professional service – slow down and then go back to the problem.

Using a journal doesn't have to mean that you diarise your daily life – it can be as simple as having an argument with yourself on paper, or just to get thoughts that you are preoccupied with, out of your own system to come back to them later. Because of the way that our brains work – writing things down physically can help with processing the emotions associated with the thoughts we are writing and so acts as an extremely powerful rehearsal tool – as if we had already experienced them. Which can provide relief and even allow for a good night's sleep when racing thoughts have been keeping you awake.

Ducks are often found in groups, and can be distracted and just follow the rest of the group without really thinking about if it's what they want.

The trouble with replicating this behaviour is that you lose sight of what you want for yourself if you get dragged into whatever the other ducks are doing too easily.

"But the rest of the ducks are doing it too..." is quite frankly, an awful excuse for not sticking to your guns. Remove it now.

Chapter Summary/Key Takeaways

- Be your future friend – what will make life easier if you plan and prepare for it?

- Simplify everything you can

- Don't be a dangerous duck!

Conclusion

Thanks for reading all the way to the end. You've made it.

I really hope you feel empowered, capable, and ready to paddle like crazy whilst remaining calm on the surface.

I would like to take this moment to remind you that **if** you feel like things are slipping you will remember to go back – take another look at what you are telling yourself. Reframe anything negative. Ponder on why you are thinking that way; is it someone else's voice penetrating your thoughts? Take ten minutes to just breathe on it.

Call a friend and get some support. That support could even be scheduling a break. In fact – go have a break now that you've finished reading. Take a bath. Write a list of all the things you'd like to do this year. Even just 5 things that you can aim for and reward yourself for working so hard to improve your life when you manage them. You deserve it.

Simplify as <u>many</u> things as possible.

If it's complicated, requires too much thinking, too many choices – chances are, you will get fed up and will not feel motivated to continue. You can do this, and feel energized, excited even about taking massive steps.

Be proud! Shout about it! Or Quack. The choice is yours entirely.

Now go and be the best, craziest, happiest, duck *you* can be.

If this book has helped you, I'd love to hear about it. You can find me on most social media or via the details further on. (#selfhelpforducks)

Useful Things:

- Write me nice messages here: hannah@soulfocuscoaching.co.uk genuinely – I'd absolutely love to hear from you and what you thought about the book if it made any difference to you. And I will do my best to get back to you.

- My website address is: www.soulfocuscoaching.co.uk/selfhelpforducks

There are links to all of the resources to be found on there, which will include:

- Daily Block Planner
- To-Do Lists
- Links to Pomodoro Timers
- Printable Goal Planners
- Self Care Planner

You can find me, my coaching, and everything else I do via the website. I am constantly learning and doing my best to grow and offer new things, from coaching to practical help preventing burnout and encouraging a more balanced approach to life and business as a parent online – so no matter where you are, I'd love to help you to get more done too.

Acknowledgments

A huge thank you to anyone who came and sat up late with me whilst I drank copious amounts of coffee typing this up.

Tracy, Bekky, and Amber; you ladies keep my world afloat all in your own way I'm lucky to have you on-side and am always grateful for your friendship and complete and utter honesty – we all know too much.

Rob, for always having sound advice. And for being an absolutely grueling taskmaster when I was fed up with typing! Thank you.

Jamie – my not so little, little brother. You will be an incredible father.

About the Author

Hannah is 30, with two children and despite a rollercoaster start to life has always done her best to find herself back on two feet.

Featured in local podcasts and media, Self Help For Ducks is an easy way to access her help in getting more done around everyday life and ensuring that you retain a level of calm whilst doing it all.

You can find her online at:

www.soulfocuscoaching.co.uk

Email her directly: hannah@soulfocuscoaching.co.uk

These details will be updated as and when the book does.

Thanks for reading.

No really, Thankyou.

Now go get quacking.

Printed in Great Britain
by Amazon